*The Miniature Room*

# WINNER OF THE 2006 T. S. ELIOT PRIZE

The T. S. Eliot Prize for Poetry is an annual award sponsored by Truman State University Press for the best unpublished book-length collection of poetry in English, in honor of native Missourian T. S. Eliot's considerable intellectual and artistic legacy.

Judge for 2006: Naomi Shihab Nye

# THE
# MINIATURE
# ROOM

## POEMS BY
## REBECCA DUNHAM

Truman State University Press
New Odyssey Series

Published by Truman State University Press, Kirksville, Missouri
tsup.truman.edu

Cover art: Pieter de Hooch, *Motherly Care* (*Mother Delousing her Child*), 1658-60. Oil on canvas. Reproduced by permission of Rijksmuseum Amsterdam, The Netherlands.
Cover designer: Teresa Wheeler
Body type: Minion Pro Adobe Systems Incorporated.
Printed by Thomson-Shore, Dexter, Michigan USA

Library of Congress Cataloging-in-Publication Data
Dunham, Rebecca, 1973-
 The miniature room / Rebecca Dunham.
  p. cm. — (New odyssey series)
Poetry.
ISBN-13: 978-1-931112-61-1 (alk. paper)
ISBN-13: 978-1-931112-62-8 (pbk. : alk. paper)
ISBN-10: 1-931112-61-4 (alk. paper)
ISBN-10: 1-931112-62-2 (pbk. : alk. paper)
I. Title. II. Series
PS3604.U54M56 2006
811'.6 —dc22
                    2006017259

The paper in this publication meets the minimum requirements of the American National Standard for Information Sciences—Permanence of Paper for Printed Library Materials, ANSI Z39.48-1992.

*For Mark*

*The minuscule, a narrow gate, opens up an entire world.*

—Gaston Bachelard

# Contents

# ACKNOWLEDGMENTS

Grateful acknowledgment is made to the editors of the following journals in which several poems in this collection have previously appeared:

*AGNI:* "A Leaf, A Hare"

*American Literary Review:* "Yard Elegy"

*Analecta:* "Poem in the Manner of Frida Kahlo"

*Bellingham Review:* "Summer"

*Beloit Poetry Journal:* "Galileo's Daughter," "The Tempest," "Catherine Blake"

*Blackbird:* "Tableau"

*Borderlands: Texas Poetry Review:* "All That Is" (as "Elegy I Do Not Wish to Write")

*Crab Orchard Review:* "Ontology of the Miniature Room," "God Measuring the World with a Compass"

*Crazyhorse:* "Phial: Elizabeth at Age 6," "Extremity"

*Cream City Review:* "Self-Portrait as Miniature"

*Dogwood:* "Black Frost"

*Elixir:* "Detail"

*Gulf Coast:* "Saint Anne to Her Daughter," "Harem of Saint Marcia"

*Hawai'i Pacific Review:* "The Soap Bubble"

*Indiana Review:* "Box Series"

*Natural Bridge:* "Ghazal in Minium"

*North American Review:* "Oxidation"

*Sycamore Review:* "Putting Him to Bed"

*Valparaiso Poetry Review:* "Two Photographs"

I am also grateful to the Wisconsin Institute for Creative Writing for the generous support that enabled the writing of many of these poems, as well as to the writing communities of Hollins University, George Mason University, and the University of Missouri. I would like to thank the readers who have provided invaluable help and encouragement during the drafting of this book: Colleen Abel, Emma Aprile, Scott Cairns, Ryan Flaherty, Steve Gehrke, Nadine Meyer, Eric Pankey, Sherod Santos, Marjorie Smith, Kate Umans, Ron Wallace, and most of all, Mark Pioli. I owe a deep debt of gratitude as well to Naomi Shihab Nye and Truman State University Press for honoring my work.

1

# Box Series

*1. Hotel de la Souris*

Attic insulation, path-coursed & mounded,
betrays the rodent nest, its denizens, as do
their droppings like tiny dashes—stray
punctuation swept into my dustpan. *Complete
beauty,* wrote Alberti, *is never found in a single
body, but is distributed in the many.* The first
container we dream our way back to must be
our mother's womb, egg-warm & flowing
round. But mice know how easily death will
admit one. Forgive them. Living & dying,
after all, amount to the same unquenchable
thirst. The glass's mouth blown a beggaring *O.*
Like a furred tongue, each dumb gray lump
I find curls in upon itself, a vowel to be
buried in dirt's gravel box. In a half-lull, I wait;
no final reflex whip-flicks forth. It will hold.

## 2. Joseph Cornell

Beauty belongs to the small. Nothing
that I have seen cannot be contained—
sublimity of starry sky, infinity, all
illusion. Burke believed we submit to what
we admire, but love what submits to us.
I believe that in each of us burns a universe,
dying down to bony relic & feather-soft
flurry of ash. The body itself a mere
casket craving the key that can unlock it.
Fill my final hold with characters mated
& strange: seashell, map, & metal spring.
Graft scrap of wallpaper to the butterfly's
stiff satin sails. Set me loose among
memory's strata, scavenger. Unmoor me.
Let me navigate this cell's secret door &
rise once more on legs made up of flower.

## 3. For Jack Gilbert

We make what we can of this world.
The barn swallow's throat feathers rust red,
a conflagration sparking off into song
liquid as water. *It is the fact of being brief, being
small & slight that is the source of our beauty,*
you say. This bird belongs to air, a welter
of jewel-like images teeming & turning,
bright swords in sunlight. *Like a wooden ocean
out of control. A beached heart.* Its raftered
nest floats, cup of mud pressed against its
own limitations like fruit to its rind.
Eggs nestle deep within, brown & white
spotted seeds. In death or birth it is
the same clay chalice rising up on all sides
that swaddles us, undowned, as we orbit
& spin through heaven's cold, open space.

## 4. *The Insistence of Geometry*

*—Melencolia I*, Dürer, 1514

I choose this life, this meager box of tools:
millstone, metaphor, polyhedron, pen.
Washed up, in a slump, I refuse your wings.
Too dog-tired to climb some ladder to God
knows where, I take the bat's webbed
hand in mine. My compass points down.
Each year this body buckles, arcs round
as I assume a newborn's sibilant shape,
rumpled & robed—a taffeta sea quite unlike
the ocean, running true as your lines' rule.
Hand of mine, the compass points down
to nowhere I would take. Battered, I am
too dog-tired to climb some ladder to God.
Washed up, in a slump, I refuse your wings,
millstone, metaphor, polyhedron, pen.
I choose this life, this meager box of tools.

# This is a Letter

This is a letter to the worm-threaded earth.

This is a letter to November, its gray bowl of sky riven by black-branched
    trees.
A letter to split-tomato skins, overripe apples, & a flock of fruit flies lifting
    from the blueing clementines' wood crate.
To the broken confetti of late fall leaves.
This is a letter to rosemary.

This is a letter to the floor's sink & creak, the bedroom door's torn hinge
    moaning its good-night.
This is to the unshaven cheek.
To cedar, mothballs, camphor, & last winter's unwashed wool.
This is a letter to the rediscovered,

to mulch, pine needles, the moon, frost, flats of pansies, the backyard,
    hunger, night, the unseen.
This is a letter to soil, thrumming as it waits to be turned.
This is a letter to compost, eggshell's bone-ash chips, fruit rinds curved like
    fingernails, & stale chunks of bread.
A letter to the intimate dark—mouth-warm & damp as a bed.

This is a letter to the planet's scavenging lips.

# THE SOAP BUBBLE

Breath-swelled planet, light swirls
wildfire up your slopes, steep
& fast. What I want to say is
something like we never die, or
fire's a visible reminder of form,
how we exchange one for the next.
Fiery tongues soft as rose petalings,
as pellicle of soap, dropped from
on high. Divinity made clear
if only I had ears to listen. I lack
humility, sense of proportion, what
I want to say consumed like flash
fuel in language's copse. The hills
burn: heat's cleansing smudge laying
ash for what's to come. Fire-whirls
tornado treetops, ignite crowns
into candelabras.  Even as I think,
the hammered sphere disappears,
thinned gold fine. What did I want
to say? *Iridescent, trace, marble, flame.*
Something plain.

# Sappho: Portrait Sitting, 1877

The Aegean slate splinters & splits.
When Mengin drew the black drape
down, baring both my breasts
to his studio's chill air, the nipples
tightened—yes, this is what it is
to be Sappho, hair's soot-thick
smear drowning small tilt of face.
Is not my corpus a corpse of sorts?
Papyrus unscrolls from my womb
like a child's paper-doll chain, limbs
& heads scissored, the rest left
for scrap. A tortoise shell, my lyre
dangles, reminds: the most common
lines, when rent, are what poetry
is made of. The *don't strip bark*
*from the evergreen* or *I'm tired* or *so much*
*cracker fell in bed last night, we'll need*
*to change the sheets.* Dwarfed by dark,
element exposed, we cast our words
out to sea to be pestled by sky's
mineral force. All that is spit back,
granular, will be what survives:
dead to light, ears pound & sweat
pours over skin's sallow grass. Bark-
tired, so much fails. Night sheets.

# PHIAL: ELIZABETH BISHOP AT AGE 6

I will not be that which scatters,
that which exists in pieces.
My mother's mind, my father's
body, whole as flocked gulls
working to tear mussel
from shell, an indeterminate
cluster of white on the break-
water's slick black. Only

to blast skyward at a child's
windmilling approach, wings
beating air. Loss: that thunder.

Ailments range my bed table,
a menagerie of glass phials.
The swell of each vessel's hull
a print of its blower's breath,
contained. On my back,
air sloshes tidal in the chest's
basin. Lungs push breath
out & take it back like a girl
swinging. I want
to house its current, to be

its phial, bright sprig of cardinal
flowering the bed.

Often, I think, my body tries
to shake me off, a long tan
tangle of housecoat.

I gather its folds about me,
its indiscretions: skin's dry scales
& jerking dance of limb.

Too weak to walk, I cannot
learn these new orbits, the path
from armoire to bed
to window. At night, I click
my flashlight off & on,
a headland beacon blinking

*I am here. I am here. I am here.*

# OXIDATION

What has been abandoned need not be
unloved or forgotten. In the far back
corner of the yard, the wheelbarrow rests
on its side, the blue paint adored

by rust, wood handles loose with use.
In winter's late-day light, I find it
beautiful as anything that's made its place,
fringed gold by embroideries of grass.

It is comfortable here in plain sight.
Rust corsets it, sides flaring like a horse's.
When the time comes, let it. Let the fine
red lace cast its veil over my insides.

# ONTOLOGY OF THE MINIATURE ROOM

If life is a stage, then props are its truest
players: minuscule harpsichords strung
with moving keys, tiny books splayed open.
It is best to hint at habitation, but not
insist. Let the slight indent of a bed's
neat coverlet conjure the prim & purring
cat, how it will sleek between candlesticks,
claws hooking the hand-stitched rugs.

Our proof of existence lies not in action,
but in the traces we leave behind. That chair
pulled out, just so. A satin green pillow
elbowed askew. To enter a room is to be
flooded by departure, by impressions fixed
upon cushion & wood in silent palimpsest.

# Artemisia Slaying Holofernes, 1620

Let men take what comfort
they can in a Judith young & lithe.
Caravaggio's girl bends, recoils
as she extracts her reedy vengeance.
Each Judith I make bears my own
visage, apron & brow gored by
paint & all its specklings, lush-
fleshed, sleeves pushed up like
a kitchen maid's. She eyes the neck
stalk, guiding her blade with care,
hand steadying his head, not afraid
to press her weight into the work.
His eyes I paint open as a fish.
Eight years later, his hand's seal
still waxes my mouth. Let his blood
wet her, let it stain her gold
dress, flaming hot, his splayed legs
visible. It is because men rape
that they cleave to the belief that
we're incapable of facing the body's
own meat. They ignore the dinner
we disembowel nightly, butter
massaged into a fowl's fatted muscle,
our fingers beneath its plucked
& dimpled skin. I want to forget,
take memory by its hair & hack,
done with it. Want to drop it
like a ham, or trophy, in my sack.

# A Leaf, A Hare

*1. Penelope*

To arrive, one learns to journey
  light, & so we molt, reptilian.
I coif seething braids of hair,
  a-hiss. Beggar red & sun roughed,
he tells of his travels. The loom
  that is his voice shuttles its tale.
Each day unravels. He chucks
  my chin, as if to say, *really?* But
this emptying defines us. Marriage
  a flaxen heap of threads upon
the floor. Not yet that morning
  I wake to alone, death's worsted
light cool as it strips him beyond
  my repair. Time's the harder course.
How could I not come to love
  the lay, its repetition, how it beats
the filling yarn into place? *Patience.*
  A leaf, a hare, still treadle into view.

## 2. Odysseus

Nothing less than the world
      tapestries her lap, a cauldron of form-
lessness for her steady fingers
      to pick amongst, calling litter
of thread to life. A leaf. A hare,
      haunches gleaming & bunched,
ready to spring across the linen's
      dun to its far border. Her lips
mouth faith. Patience. What
      was I to do when her chill body
held itself so distant? Root about,
      mud-mucked, until night's aching
riptide dragged me down, only
      to be retched back up on that
sandy shore? Her webbed face
      unreadable. A troop of swine
issues from her loom. Fidelity is
      a witch's craft. What was I to do?

## 3. Duet

Time is the harder course.
  A cauldron of formlessness, each
day unravels. Her chill body
  held itself so distant. I wake alone,
ready to spring across this
  empty night's aching riptide,
its repetition, how it beats. Is
  fidelity nothing less than the world,
a flaxen heap of threads upon
  the floor? A leaf, a hare tapestries
her lap. We molt, marriage
  a witch's craft beyond my repair.
It strips him, haunches gleaming
  & bunched reptilian. How could
I not come to love her fingers,
  mouth, & lips? What was I
to do? Arrive, seething, on that
  sandy shore, dun to its far border.

2

# EXTREMITY

—*Study of God the Father,* 1555–1560

His hands rubbed blood-
bright, Primaticcio struggled

to bring forth a man in his own
image, the kind of monster
who'd hoard holy relic & limb.

These nine muscled arms all
that he could manage.

A hand surfaces, wrist up,
palm flat as a waiter's beneath
his dinner-laden tray. Like

a worm chopped to pieces,
caught & scattered, the segments
curve amid death's
throes on his pinked tablet.

Faith is a grisly contest.

This portrait devours sight.
Eyes awash in the body's
red, it casts itself over my retinas—
phantom green flood, a prayer
to ligament & gristled limb.

The hand makes the man.
I recognize him:

God the Braggart, God the Afflicted,
God who Holds-the-Line.
God the Tempter.
His fingers reach for mine.

# Ghazal in Minium

The powder is poison, red heavy, earth. I write what I see, St. Hildegard
said. Flames erupt from her forehead, flood her brain, heart, & breast.

Like two pears wrapped in tissue, the breasts reveal themselves.
Like cold & sculpted stone, they desire breath upon their skin.

The disease woman crouches beneath her diagnoses. Never say fear fuels
the hypochondriac, but passion. Life softens & she clutches tighter. *More.*

Like a pale sack filled with rocks, the skin of the engorged breast smarts.
Like a sunburst, stretch marks flare cinnabar, rays from her nipple.

*Self-Portrait in the Letter R:* Remember, straight head & spine. Imagine
your vertebrae as beads on a string that runs to the ceiling, to a hand unseen.

# Winter Solstice

The sun stands in place,
unable to stir above the slight
green smudge of horizon.

We rise with our only son
to see the longest night stretch
far past the second black

cup of coffee & shower. Frozen
to the stoop, a robin's body,
neat as a gift. Starlings shift

inside sky's gray dish, loose
iron filings. The curtain lifts.
All is turbid dawn-blur, drizzle-

rigged, as the earth tips back in its
boiled-wool cover, dead flint.
Stiff & sparkless, it reminds me

this is the season of stillness.

# TABLEAU

*1. Christmas Eve*

On the mantel, this silent scene, motionless
amid the heat expelled by our hearth's open

cave. Fire's chiaroscuro spit & clamor
strikes the figures' porcelain robes where

they hang in folds, crevice of throat & eye
sunken coal. The trough's straw-sculpted

maw fills with dark, empty until midnight.
This créche should embody beginnings,

holy birth, but the darkness to come
inhabits it too thoroughly. See how it slips

into the stable—the cattle low & stamp
the stalls, trapped by massing smoke. Their

hooves paw kilned dirt. Only one man need
notice, need lift the bolt & slide it free:

let them nose their way out, break for safety.

*2. The Adoration*

whether on your knees or squatting

to worship is to labor, as any saint knows

in water or walking

let love pour forth from you, wetting both your socks

then rest & push again

faith is like that, one step forward, one step back

keep your chin down

(that which is distant is all that is worth seeing)

whether on your side, your back

the posture of adoration is the posture of suffering.

## 3. The Nativity

Snow swirls the night air like a nebula
& already he is lost, retiring to grottoed barn.

He tosses on his makeshift bed
before rising for work, worried about taxes
unpaid, the donkey to be fed, & when
he'll get a decent night's rest.

He has seen enough of open sky & stars.

He wants the splintered crisscross of beams,
material he can hew according to desire,
wants to lift his thumb to her teeth
& have her tweeze each wood sliver free.

*4. The Epiphany*

A thin music's strain accompanies the infant's every breath.

The branchings of his lungs stiffen, heavy as tree limbs
outside, fragile bouquets of twig piled thick with old snow.

Censerlike, the vaporizer offers up its menthol, its mist.

I have known nothing so well as I know this wet face,
its veins tracked like bird's feet across earth's white crust.

## 5. Candlemas

Knead loaves of bread with milk & holy
water to place beneath spring's first furrow.

Plant garden seeds in an egg carton. Wait.

Warm them on the kitchen counter—
green shoots flicker on soil's black lake.

Sweep the floors with salt water. Batter &

pour a dinner of pancakes, round gold disks.
Kindle soft candles, beeswaxed stars,

in every window. This is how light must enter

our world: sharp & bright as a sword,
suns blister-cupped by a woman's

corded arms, consuming her like a wick.

# CARTOGRAPHY OF THE SUBLIME

It does not take a mountain to lift
the human soul. A distant train's dirge,
winter's brief thaw leaking the bluff's

sides, trees reefed & skeletal, a simple
recognition & something quickens, even
as we flounder, swine in this land's trough.

Transport seekers, spiny haired & mud
spattered, who is to say the way is up?

# Black Frost

Next door,
the dark fruits revolve & fall.

When you give up hope
in godliness, there's not much point
to keeping clean—

let them dirty themselves,
let the chill night run
its black cloth
across their skin.

Somebody's always done for.
It's just like we said,
just like the thin line of ants
snaking our walls,
every line leading back to the same
sweet poison, three clear
tears on the strip
ripped from a cereal box.

Remember:
the cold has no voice
& our neighbor will sleep for days.

It can only be
the intercom swarming,
buzzing *we have come so far
it is over.*

The oven opens its mouth,
the last thin blue towel
folded in fourths
& placed on the rack
to pillow our nap.

Let the paramedics serve
as pallbearers, they are
accustomed

to the cold body
with its shock of dead hair
unwashed for days,
strands black

as the apples dangling
from our neighbor's tree.

# Poem in the Manner of Frida Kahlo

—after *What the Water Gave Me*, Kahlo, 1938

A volcano's searing ring haloes the skyscraper's glass & metal skin.
In a boa of smoke, it sinks, flame-licked. Sheets of ash shower the sky.

*Some crookedness is in this thing. Have no faith,* the obstetrician says, as if
he grapples giant eels. I never knew how much blood there could be.

Rust needles give way beneath my rubber-soled boots, the sun seeping
in clots. Pines rise thin & black, spoking into furred stars overhead.

Or will it go like this: stooping, I lift the wooden bowl. Inside, absence
sticky as its curves. & out, smooth & beautiful as a finely-sanded skull.

Weeping willow branches snake through the park's matted grass &
I watch a boy haul one free, only to brandish its length like a whip.

The bathwater cools. With a toe, I open the drain. Muscles & cords pull
taut, still, as I listen to its noisy emptying, my body laid out in the tub.

# Self-Portrait as Miniature

What a wafer of a casket, this ivory
oval strung about your neck. Beneath
the covering glass, my hair
gleams light as a ghost's. Bend close.
I am meant for no one. But you,
I fit the palm of your hand.
Think not of the strap that secured
my slack jaw or the way each sitting

decomposed me. Turn me
around. Ever facing inward—
my limned flesh warm as the chest
where I rest—you must approach me
as you would a secret. I whisper.

# CURATOR OF FRUIT

*—Isabella Dalla Ragione, arboral archaeologist*

It is the old women I love
    most, the remembered
piles of pear, plum, apple,
    cherry, peach, medlar,
& quince that they cellared
    beneath their nuptial beds,
where it was cool. How I want
    to possess the smell
& taste of all that's past,
    to graft scion & rootstock,
bind them tight. I desire
    life itself, to turn my land
heavy with musked
    orbs of imperfect fruit.
A rutted road thrusts over
    potato fields to the Fiorentina
tree, black-freckled pear,
    its bark split & gowned
in a lichen intricate white.
    The life I've chosen is not
my own. I know that many
    could say the same: the trees,
blushing old women.
    It is no cause for complaint.
Marriage is a stony bed,
    is want. Inedible flesh

bagged in its spotted skin,
      the sap's inexplicable rise
to sky, & early morning, love
      heavy with the smell of winter
pears, firm & crisp & cold.

3

# Putting Him to Bed

*1.*

Bath steam coats us, whiting's sifted
dust. The girdled sun bores down
as night collects like cuttlefish ink
in the heavens' glazed bowl. *If you
take away the light all things remain
unknown in the shadows,* said St. John
of Damascus. My son agrees. I must
be Byzantine, must don a visage
chromed to green, must let no pity
escape my constant eyes. Though
*no one may enter that place, there
are many rooms as to surpass all belief,*
or so I have read, in sleep's palace.
Yolk of me, it is past 8 o'clock,
& I just cannot read one more story.

*2.*

I close my son's bedroom door,
lamp-black rectangle in a wall pale
as pulped linen, as cotton rag.
Back curved, knees tucked to chin,
my husband floats the sofa's swell,
a bright segment of tangerine. What
we feel for each other during this
is best left unsaid. Of his unicorns
Marco Polo wrote: *on their tongues,*
*in fact, they have long sharp spines.*
How to say thank you, how to be
thankful? It must be something like
what an explorer feels for sleep,
finally closing her eyes to the stars'
strange array. The old blanket's
weft reassuring, familiar on feet
that seek out another's in darkness.

*3.*

*Sleep with me,* my son begs. I lie down
beside him & dark's fingers mold our skin,
a study in stasis. The terror of the formless
surrounds us. Horror is just another
mother of beauty: the Grand Khan's palace
dome that *glitters like crystal & can be seen
shining from a great way all around* bought
at the cost of nights populated by nutria,
distorted trees, & toads staring with goggled
eyes. I have no wonders to offer. Just
my body, immobile earth caught by
this blue palpitation, the moon's pilot light.

*4.*

*Sleep with me,* he says, the sibilant *s*
a serpent twining through the margins
of the room, sinuous as any Venetian
canal the young Marco straddled
& rode. The clock's luminous face
a verdigris moon lipped in gold leaf.
Stuffed cotton batting's animal lumps
all that lie between him & *a sea*
*so tempestuous, it is continually eating away*
*the land & scooping out trees at the root.*
Remember to retrieve all manner
of curiosities. Khan-like, I wait
arbored in rose breath. I cannot follow.

# In Which I am
# the Serpent in the Garden

Our saucer magnolia sloughs its heavy petals,
pink flurries edged with dark.
                              Its blossoms
sag open, freighted with a rich perfume.

My son, not yet two, heaps them back atop
the lowest-hanging blooms. What is it like,

to live unencumbered by death, unhemmed
by certitude? Mortality presses & fences—

I fear most the clear field, its carelessness,
childhood's feral innocence, & its cruelty.
On our stoop, a daddy longlegs
                              drawn & quartered.
The thread of its leg quivers.

Knowledge is the apple's humble gift.

He needs to see the way brown pulls itself up
over the moist white flesh, like a sheet.

I pluck an apple from the fruit bowl & slice it,
luminous, a fan of moons flowering his plate.

# STILL LIFE WITH GILT GOBLET

We are not unlike this
opened meal's wet insides:
a dinner roll's gilded crust
broken, the glass
tipped, a single lemon
sliced & peeled in infinite
spiral of rind, tablecloth
jostled, the platefuls
of mollusk cracked wide—

the Dutch knew much
about the body, arrested
& rent in their attempt
to paint the soul,
to disclose the oyster
by its watery light alone.

# Vernal Equinox

The forsythia explodes, a struck
match. Branches tindered by
wind betray my desire, my long
canary love. A hundred flamey
mouths unfurl, petal & spark
arcing down: what it feels like
to give & burn. I want to catch,

kindled, into bundles of hard
yellow buds—arms & legs, even
the loose strands of my hair fire-
working out. I want to break
into blossom, my limbs flailing
in air's current like a man on fire.

# BOOK OF THE CITY OF LADIES

## 1. Annunciation of Christine de Pizan

I slouch over my chair's pommeled
arm, shut up by edifice of word.
Each illuminated leaf makes of a page
a box & makes of a book a room.
The texts tower about me, peopled
by women devilish & wicked. I am
famished, a monstrosity in nature.
How can I revel in the simple gasp-

grasp of my appetites? When will
my good mother call me to my dinner?
Day's last rays finger my lap. Tumblers
rattle, revolving—the click of metal
gear on metal fills me & releases,
fierce as the key-sure light, fitted tight.

## 2. Christine de Pizan, Laying Brick

Daphne, Dorothy, Rebecca, Anne,
Gertrude, & the Magdalen—

waist high, the city wall wimples.
Each joint must be watertight,
handmaid Reason reminds, lest
my project be lost to winter's snap
& freeze, lest my labor be stillborn,
a lifeless wheeze. Vermilion lakes
blister my palm. I butter bricks
& shove them into mortar's bed:

Sappho, Catherine, Artemisia, Eve,
Marcia, Lilith, Hildegard, & me.

# DETAIL

*—The Virgin with the Veil*, Raphael


Not the veil, but the fingers that hold it.
My son winds himself in our sliding
door's sheer drape. His fists stretch it
as if punching some taut membrane
from his face. This is our game:
he turns in his cocoon & I unghost him.
Frozen mid-act, the fabric
rasps my finger's pads. He laughs.
My hand still remembers our early
nights, the careful ritual of wrapping.
I would tuck the white blanket
tight, his arms folded in like wings.
*Sleep.* Not the veil waiting to be shaken
free, a handkerchief's bright flash,
but the fingers. It is terrible. Not
the veil, but the fingers that must hold it.

# CATHERINE BLAKE

I flush my paintbrush against the water bowl's sides.
A cloudy tail spirals up in its wake. For me,
each morning dawns to a disk of fire not unlike
a guinea, & this he will not forgive. My paper

glows out yellow like the sun rising & singing
to my husband: *Holy, Holy, Holy, the Lord God*
*Almighty!* A swarm of angels crying to him,
he says, & though I try to see otherwise, it's just

the bees that have roosted in our eaves. The dry
husks of their bodies bat the window panes.
I dip my brush's tip & swirl it round
a lozenge of paint. Only here, in the window's

mirror glare, do I see more than he:
white feathers spit from my lips instead of air,
sticking to me, a gutted pillow's snowy innards,
til I am waxed & feathered as any saint here.

# THE TEMPEST

Clouds orchard the sky, dangle
flush globes overhead. The storm
has not passed. There is no
rest, I know, just my son's cry

splintering the silence. A flash
both serpentine & bright.
If sleep's slick waters could slip
their banks & cover me

like a sheet. If the telephones, tea
kettle, even the rasping green
sofa's slipcovered twill could be
quieted. Below the water's purled

surface, a stillness pours. Please.
This, the uninhabited moment.

# SAINT ANNE TO HER DAUGHTER

—*Madonna & Saint Anne,* Leonardo Da Vinci

It will not work. He'll never
fold back into you, body curled
tight, a kitten in sleep. He leans—
seems always to lean—away.
Everything you do pulls death, thick
& woolly, closer to your emptied
flesh. There is room. Skin sags
your shrunken belly. Remember:

there is always room now
for death to clamber into your lap,
heavy as a child & bleating.
It's in your weight on my legs. The last
prickings of sensation fade, numb
as when you first emerged, smudged
with blood & vernix. I knew:
the fingers tipped with blue.

4

# HAREM OF SAINT MARCIA

*—Marcia Painting Her Self-Portrait,* 1403

In this studio, I have been licked & loved,
awash in oil, have known her brush's
muzzled flick & tease. She does only women,
stroking curve of breast & dimpled thigh.
In life, we are chambered saints, framed flat
as flowers left to lean against her wall.
Pots & palette arrayed, she paints my nuptial
face. Please, good lady, extend your hand
to mine—we are virgin merely as men define.
& you, so well-versed, must be past ready
to die. Hungry for the grave, I am duplicitous,
image piled on image, oval glass & panel.
Lay me across your chest. Casketed in that bed,
I will minister you until your back curls
& dark slides over in its long & final scrape.

# Reptilian Nocturne

I sleep with my eyes open as anyone
of sense. Night rivers about me
as I sink below its surface & lurk.
Let the devout trust darkness.
I have seen the cat's brood, burlap
sacked. Have seen how the hot
bodies of the faithful worm, mewling,
blind in that bag's belly like a many-
headed monster. *The crocodile is*
*the image of the hypocrite.* Fine. Call me
what you will. Better a pretender
than the kittens, the fisted rock,
or the hand that releases its burden
to black water. *Our father who art*
*in heaven.*

# GALILEO'S DAUGHTER

Father, I send you this electuary of fig,
nut, rue leaves, & salt.

A plague beats our convent gates.

Crystals of arsenic burn at my wrist
& float in my lap's jet folds.

If your silhouette were to scorch
the parchment sheet hung between us
I would know what a woman knows,

curtained within her bed, when
the black form of her lover approaches.

# Two Photographs

—Vietnam, 1969

*1.*

None of them look the camera in the eye.
Center: a stack of new fatigues
fills one man's arms. Far left: my uncle,
helmet cupping his skull. I know him
because the caption reads *Bruce—*
*in background with back to camera.*
The other two men seem more vulnerable,
heads bare & exposed, dark clipped
hair coming to a point. Aim here.
All four men keep eyes cast down, bodies
mimicking the attitude of prayer. They look
their enemy in the eye, learn its lush
green face, the undulating earth
that would take them in a wet embrace.

*2.*

Their backs are all we see. Single file
the line of men snakes through foreground's
flat grasses toward green hills, slopes
gentle as burial mounds. One of the men
humping gear is my uncle, machine
gun in hand. I've forgotten which. Their backs
are all I see. *Am I crazy,* my father said, *or
are the back of his head & ears unmistakably
Bruce?* I study the image, the shadow of ears
protruding from each man's helmet.
My uncle has no face. We are unable to
remember. This is how it happens,
how features erode, interchangeable as
a set of ears. Their backs are all I can see.

# ALL THAT IS

There's a bit of Chinese emperor in us all.
Of daily details, I have a thousand—

this butter-scraped piece of toast,
its crusts scattered like tea leaves
in the gentle indent of my breakfast plate—

all interred in language's tomb like
life-sized battalions of terra-cotta men.

I will admit to knowing Qin's desire
to contain a life with one great wall,
jeweled sky chandeliered over mercury

rivers guarded by infantry & archer.
But such cavalry can bring no comfort.

Better to let you rock back, neglected
& unfixed in this earth's cold bed,
to leave you to the soil's rooted arms.

Let them pull you up so you fly apart
& flower me with all that is pink inside.

# GOD MEASURING THE WORLD WITH A COMPASS

—Illumination in a moralized Bible, ca. 1250

Blue-fleshed fingerlets, uneven as a shoreline,
reach up into dark space from wavy rind.

If God *must needs have made things according*
*to number, weight, & measure,* then he must be

troubled by the chaos cross-sectioned
beneath his instrument's sharp points, the curved
contours of this planet's bulging body,

cosmos circumscribed by two hinged legs
like a cantaloupe halved upon my counter.

I scoop sticky seed & fiber free.

We are so small. Beauty's daily disarray of vine
straggles my garden's weed-pocked patch.

Sun glazed, the irregular globes of melon swell.

# WINNOWING

*Parrotia, hosta, portulaca, spiderwort's eight-*
*legged blooms.* His toy robin vised to chest,
my son wrings mechanical song from down
stuffing. *False spirea, paper bark maple, daisy,*
*the Louisa crab.* Even in his sleep, I hear
when he clutches her, hear her inky fluting
tossed to the night. My own flocked
words are dun lumps fitted to the body's
rookery. Are warm balls of dough. *Weeping*
*cherry, lavender twist, Oklahoma redbud,*
*fringe.* All I do is press. *Impatiens, hornbeam,*
*black-eyed Susan.* Their soft & feathery
fan blows open, emerging from throat's
shadow like a bird breaking for open sky.

# Yard Elegy

*1.*

The Midwest's humid bowl fills, laboring
my movements. Slender stalked,

the peonies stoop under ponderous blooms.
Their profusion of ruffle rivals any gown.

Within each flower, tiny ants cluster
& pillage for sugar, peeling the tissue-thin

petals of each balled bud. This must be
how life reveals us, nudged imperceptibly

by the slightest heft, until the soul
slips free in deathbed's thick sweetness.

A single vase can suffuse a room,
its ineluctable scent sacking the body,

as if to talcum it violet, rose. On the table
beside my head, the bouquet, in lush repose.

*2.*

Like the rinds of a lime, a hinged moon, or
a four-eyed augur of death,

the luna moth clings to my window screen,

hind wings flaring & mouthless—
she is as she was meant to be,
perfect & light as air, her inevitable demise
made manifest in her very design—

but such intimacy with death, its bright sickle,

is too much, so I turn out the light
& let the moon hook night's distant velum,

my own end cocooned within me.

*3.*

The pink curl of another nestling lies
dead on our drive, wrinkled &
featherless. I lift it in a clutch of towels,

then drop it in the trash. Death
is as close as the next strong gust, as easily

opened as our front door, the damp
predawn grass cooling my son's feet.

Such a fine threshold—the rim of a nest,
the line where lawn ends & the street's dim
grave stretches wide. The young

are drawn to edges, to the place where
beams of light bear down upon them.

## 4.

Like a lady shedding her stays, the maple's bark drops away.

Like house lights doused, room by room, the mimosa fails:
 last year one limb & this year two, branches that never
 split into leaf, never bloom.

Like the desire that follows a jealous fire, the sapling's foliage
 flares, withers, & falls—only to unfurl again before
 August, & then no more.

Like a pregnant belly, the infested stem of each cottonwood
 leaf, aphid-choked, breaks & sinks in a slow green rain.

5.

Everywhere, death. The clod of cat
dung I sift from the sandbox barrow,

that inch of standing water deposited
by last night's rain in my son's pool,

new mushrooms spreading their soft
gray umbrellas over our yard. I know

that I cannot protect him, even as
I latch him tight in his swing & push

until the tips of his sneakers brush
the pear tree's leaves. He squeals—

the vowels break from his open throat
in violent delight, soaring—not,

I imagine, unlike the final moment
when the soul bursts into flower.

The swing's red bucket tolls back &
forth, carrying him with it, in rapture.

# SUMMER

— after the painting by Giuseppe Arcimboldo, 1573

poses, in profile, face composed of plump
orbs resembling muscle & ligature
stripped of skin, baroque as a greengrocer's
pile—pears, plums, cherries, & garlic
with the split shell of pea for a mouth.
*Summer is what it is,* God says. Vegetable heaps
spill from plastic crates, & farmers shove
handfuls of green bean, potato, & leek
into paper bags. I pace our market's stands,
seeking ripest tomato, sweetest peach,
berry pints so plush they burst on the tongue.
*See,* they say, giving themselves over, life
laid out before me like a proof.  How to bear
what must follow? *It is what it is,* God insists.
Arcimboldo's portrait lashes, it scoffs.
No, I say to open air, to the sheathed
pyramids of moist green corn. Wit makes
more of this than overripe display, dissected
& arranged. It is what it is. Call it solace.

# NOTES

In section 3 of "Box Series," the lines in italics are from *Refusing Heaven* by Jack Gilbert.

In "Black Frost," several phrases are from poems by Sylvia Plath.

The italicized phrase in "Poem in the Manner of Frida Kahlo" is spoken by Laocoön in Virgil's *Aeneid*.

"Curator of Fruit" is indebted to John Seabrook's article on Isabella Dalla Ragione in *The NewYorker*, September 5, 2005.

"Putting Him to Bed" quotes Marco Polo's *The Travels*.

The first italicized phrase in "Reptilian Nocturne" is from the twelfth century *Cambridge Bestiary*.

In "God Measuring the World with a Compass," the italicized portion comes from Bonaventure of Bagnoregio's *Commentary on the Four Books of Sentences,* as translated by Umberto Eco in *History of Beauty*.

# About the Author

Rebecca Dunham is assistant professor of English at the University of Northern Iowa. Awards include the Jay C. and Ruth Halls Poetry Fellowship, the 2005 Indiana Review Poetry Prize, and a 2005 Academy of American Poets Prize. She received her PhD in creative writing from the University of Missouri-Columbia.